Richard

Old Stones New Tales

old stones new tales

poems by richard douglas pennant

MAKIRIMA BOOKS
MMVI

First published 2004 by Makirima Books
Penrhyn
Bangor
Gwynedd LL57 4HN
Wales

Printed and bound by
Aristos Philis Printers Ltd, Limassol
Cyprus

ISBN 0-9547722-0-2

To all those who made the difference.

May our shared memories not forget us,
last lifetimes,
and our dreams become the legends
of lifetimes to come.

Acknowledgements

In the first instance, this book has had a five-year gestation period, since chronologically it represents, with one or two more recent exceptions, the earliest of my poetry that I have kept. However, it has been over thirty years since I first started writing. Of those intervening years virtually nothing survives. For whatever reason, I tended to consign to the waste paper basket nearly all my creative work. Yet, it was wholly due to a wiry little French Canadian, Jean Paul Cretain, that I began writing at all. His inspired teaching gave me the courage to explore what was in my soul, and to write of what I found there. He is the first person I must thank.

I would like to thank my family and friends for their gentle persuasion to press on, and not only to write, but to keep what I had written, and not throw it away; Giorgia, Pamela and Yiannis, thank you all for your patience and support.

I must especially thank Rosa and Stephen Somerville, Elwyn Roberts and Glenys Lloyd and her husband Will; all of whom read the book in its manuscript form, and who advised and encouraged.

I must not forget my dear friends Dr Eleni Rossides and her husband Nick who gave me many hours of their time helping me in my quest to understand myself better.

Yet, my deepest thanks I save for my two 'Guardian Angels' who over the past five or six years have watched over me, nurturing, leading and inspiring. It is to you that this book is dedicated.

Richard Douglas Pennant
Limassol, May 2004

Contents

POET TO POET

(To Elwyn Roberts, with thanks)

I observed
as you held my words
in a half nelson;
loose-leaf, limp bound,
the manuscript bent double
and folded back
across its spine,

And you read me aloud
frog marching my own
ideas past me,
and for the first time,
I understood what
the rumblings in my soul
sound like;
and the shape my thoughts
take in someone else's mouth.

Then you put my feelings down
and picked up a sheaf of papers
— all yours; you gave me
a reading of what was
going in inside your mind.

I heard every word,
looked up to the oak beams
that crossed, re-crossed the ceiling;
they listened intently as well.
Then as they creaked,
your home shifted slightly,
finding a more comfortable
posture in relation
to the wind outside.

You had read me
— and yourself —
before letting me go;
with good luck for a wish
on the shake of a hand ...

11-11-11

Cenotaphs brush winter leaves aside
and squalls recall their fallen
in sudden storms,
November weeps, and cold;

A twenty-five pounder suddenly calls
a widow to falteringly place
a 'poppy-ed' cross, arrowhead to soil;

Wreathes bleed huge circles for the dead
— and the silence;

It's the silence after the scream,
now the tears — nearly everybody has lost somebody.

Now it's the peace that's hard to find
and a sniper's bullet makes it harder yet,
shot through the heart.

A bird swooned in its ecstatic circles of flight
high in the cold clear air;

That the acropolis mourned,
its past humbled, tumbled,
into a rage, ragged with stone;

History's shattered shadows
now on bended knee,
kneeling among their ruins;

And weeping ...

The piercing cry etched into the wind swoops
upon winter's lightly feathered wings;

The cry of a bird, high in its flights of fancy.

A pigeon preened — careened —
early morning's conflicting greens,
as creeping spring rising up bare bark
unwraps the sap over which
foams the apple;
and flooding cherry
scantily drapes moist ground;
lays damp night to rest,
and breaks the shroud of
fragile — crystal — cold
against the Mistle Thrush's song.

A SUMMER MORNING

A morning of silk
uncoils its oceans
running into sun
and weaves in
tireless — tide-less — waking
that golden thread
now slipping out to sea.

And the sleeping palms
— remembered —
of the night before;
where, in the darkness
they gathered ashore,
they drew in
and stooped around
the promises
secret lovers made.

Vows shared
and broken
in the kiss that told all
to the silence of the night
— beyond that
war of words
the broken hearted
left behind, rancid in the air;

They are shadows now,
of the night they've outgrown
— shadows seared into
the scalding stone we walk,
morning dripping from our brow.

AN OLD MAN AT THE BANK

It was an old war
he remembered.

The slow deliberate tones
played out in syllables
carefully chosen,
cut into the
business of the day.

Although speaking
to no one — in particular —
the room courted
then traced
each word he cast,

Across concrete
mellowing into faces,
office walls catching hard,
the loneliness of an old age;

Haunting the memories
we too shall want to share
with a world
which has grown weary
of the past.

And turning, he left,
the slow strides
of a soldier's memories
ushering out his
friends in arms
— battle weary with age —

The cordite resting
on the last words he said,
the door closing on
the one final
shell burst;

Shuffling into a sheaf
of papers.

AN ORCHARD

Trees nurse their garden walls,
red brick pruned back
to rusting wire,
nailing summers to frail mortar
along which fruitful limbs
— carefully tended —
stretch beneath the ripening sky;

Till the season passes
and the last fall of fruit
sours into showers
and the walls bow in onto
the orchards they keep;
of unkempt grass
long with summer walks.

Overstretching the capping stones
the trees catch the wind's cutting edge
and the sodden cloud dragged
down to earth sinking
into lawns and leaves
— the squandered gold
autumn leaves for winter
to kick aside.

And the trees nurse their garden walls
as best they can,
unpicked to naked trunks
bare wood, bearing the winter well,
till spring in her lush innocence
feels the colour back into
the earth's frigid limbs.

AND YES;

will you,
would you still love me;
as we watch
our first kiss
feint into middle age,

and become grey and lined,
and a little forgetful?

and you?
will you,
would you still love me
                    then ...
                              then ...

Are we such illicit friends,
we must hide our words
behind excuses,

And search out those silences
only true friendship understands;
deep within shadows shared?

The stealing out from
our safe hiding places
— this our unbroken bond —

We face our farewells
— us parting friends —
which give us back to
the angry noises of the world;

Till a greeting kiss
brings home the stillness,
the quiet between our words;

The silence only true friends
know how to share.

AT AMATHOUNDA

I

Searches the soul
the voice that carries with it
the wind across land
now standing back
in wounded awe.

Where the dust
had settled
those last — lost — words,
now 'un-buried',

And with them
the seething ground yields;

Its wild run
of earth
stopped short — rent —
into crooked banks.

Now the past
can see what
the future holds
— in scorn —
for it.

II

Spring breaches
surprising its barren sky
— blue bursting —
into stooping gallantries.
The Splash!

In this morning's sheer leap
into pools of stones,
a raw sun trawls,

And ripples across
soiled — spoiled — mosaic.

III

The broken vow,
melting now,
silence to a whisper
the smile that
over the wings of the breeze,
benigns.

Those many robed memories
'un-swept' from the shadows;
now the secrets shared
in dreams.

AUTUMN WINTER

She caught the scent of summer tiring
and ran him to earth in autumn's dappled light;
the leaves that paved the way for rainier days,
and those long evenings, shrinking — retreating —
into mornings panting — tired —
waking in wisps of breath.

Now the rains devour and deluge
the sunny corners melting to mud,
and brazened teeth gnaw into his carcase
which had for so many months
carried us on his lithe shoulders
to the silent skies above;
hamstrung has fallen helpless
beneath leafless trees.

Soon the frost in sepulchre white entombs,
carves soft ground, hard as sculptures,
and decays the corpse of evening walks.
Then sweeping rains on the hoof
idle across the acres of dormant land.
Catches the cold and turns the roads to ice.

Hangs her head, now the hunt is over
belly full of past summers' ripeness.
The rest lies trodden underfoot.
Her pride diminishes, too, as shorter days
eat into what little she has left
— now winter has come and is here to stay.

BROKEN WINGS OF A POET

Have I gate-crashed
someone's private party
or;
have you really
drawn me from the shadows?

And let the space between us
speak my name,
the music take
me by the hand.

Can you really
heal these,
my broken wings?

Turn this poet's voice
— whispering in the dark —
into song.

Can you
— can you really?

You who've shown me
each single step
across those patient
— listening — tiles,
now smooth
with other people's dance.

Can you really
— make me fly
— walk on water
... can you?

Turn this poet's voice to song.

Stir the dark waters
of my soul—to wine.

If I believe you can
— then you have.

But, its believing
in who I am,
that brings my steps
into time.

DANCING CLASSES

I measured my steps
each one counted to its time,

The music somewhere far away,
somewhere lost at the back of my mind,
that dusty place — the corner that is
those things I still have to understand.

* * *

And I will dance this slow
Zeimbekiko — Hasapiko —
to the privacy of our mirrored walls;

Till one day you will give
wings for my feet,

And watch me fly.

DOIRANA

The hills divide the spoils
of men gone mad
and the grand plans
that bled the winter
to death here,
in the scowling snows
of the Salonika Front;
home of gods
fallen to Earth;
and with the
mortal fallen among the ruins,
a lonely hillside
in shell-shocked silence,
lays September to rest.

DUSK ... and the flight of the bat ...

The flickering of night against the dark.

Velvet drawing in from the sea.

The bat that skips about the sleeping palm,
shuffling into shape around evening's
quiet words — unspoken thoughts —

And gently sweeps aside — brushes past —
the indiscretions love holds up
to a summer now into shadows slipping;

Darkened to murmur of voices,
dusk entwines in flesh the secrets
lips sustain against the quieting colours.

As raises its one last glorious cup — this hour —
releases its pasts — its stones —
to their scented promise;

Where the city swills its lights around
the dregs of the day and its short skirts
step out in search of night.

And cleaving the heavy air, hung low,
that piercing flight of velvet,
flickers the bat against the dark;

As night succumbs to human passion.

DUSK SYRIA

The afternoon tired of colour,
shed its sun carefully;
and bowing to February's
last teasing chill of winter,
marooned its hills, darkly
cut across the setting sky.

Day narrowed,
and town and village
flickered into furtive electricity ...

Lights the hillsides lifted,
trophies reaped
from the coffers of the night,
still subdued in fading light.

And scattered across
the sleepy sand,
the fumbling cold
tripped about the dark,

Feeling for our body heat,
our company
in the cold
discomfort of the dusk —

This strange beauty's
searing cold
across our nature.

From the shadows friends emerge
bringing the night along with them;
passing couples kissing,
the music turns away
and fills the dance floor.

A capacity evening.

Young feet step into
a parquet party
the strobe striking at
youthful limbs,
with its tangled light.

As tiredness sinks
to the bottom of
the drained hourglass
and the sleep that waits
among the sands.

GOODBYE

(For Pamela)

You flitted away ...
hair in a dance of autumn breeze,
and a scuttle of leaves
lying low — till now —
tripped about your feet
to fall wounded in puddles
of this morning's rain.

And you kissed your childhood goodbye
— a hurried last minute kiss —
one that says goodbye and is gone
in youth's fast — vast — energy.

But my forehead
bears the moistness still;
you the woman
and the child I've known;
now somehow wiser
in a world that still likes
to hug its teddy bears ...

in the lonely moments
when eyes don't pry.

GROWING OLD TOGETHER

These seven ages
grown old
with the decades
look back on selves
barely recognized;

The man —
the years which lined
the face once met,
and knew for an age
— or so it seemed —

Or glimpsed perhaps,
a phase, just in passing,

Recall these people
we once liked, once loathed,
but grew used to
under our skin
and close to the soul,

Bearing still the child
we never really
laid to rest;
to peer from the mirror
back at us.

Through these seven ages
we've let grow old grow cold,
and call us the names
we've got used to;

In this life time
— at least.

HIGH IN WINTER

You took me up
to the canopies of the gods,
those places of high cloud
come down to earth;
and we peered
over the parapets of cold

— and felt the forest shiver.

Birdsong crouched
cut into stone; low,
where summer waits,
lost beneath the snows
where spring has climbed
as far as it breathlessly can;
and lies curled among
a few feint fallen leaves.

Majestic this cold
that bears upon our thoughts
and in our uncertain
tufts of breath.

HOLIDAY RESORT OUT OF SEASON

As a last resort
the sun hangs on for dear life
to autumn's better days,

And now mourns
the summer's scramble
back up the mountains
it melted down.

Its beach toys in decline, wilt,
and deflated bob — hobble —
jilted by a lithe wave
of wind blown sand,
cutting its course
across the seaside roads.

Cold winds to follow
brace the place
for September's rains.

Now distinctly middle aged, this place,
and stout around the waist,
trudges in slow varicose gasps
towards December's darker days.

(For Mum)

I love gardening, you said;

I know, I remember you knee deep
in damp autumns, drizzly praying into
beds of clogged earth;

Trowelling at weeds till the light
going, went, and brought you in
to tea, sherry, and Evening Primrose.

I love gardening, you said;

I know, and you told me why;
a gardener always looks forward, you said;
to another day, another season,
that next patch of clear sky
and there to work in.

That's why, you said;
as you toiled towards your next tomorrow
— until that next winter came,
and, so quickly, took you.

IN MEMORIAM

Bright the stars
this cloudless night
keeps vigil with your grief,

Those silent constellations
store the secrets
of the broken hearted
in the cavernous
belly of the night.

While a golden moon
looks down,
tears shed like stars
fall from the broken
depths of the night.

Breaking onto
that last goodbye
— the farewell —
even unsaid perhaps.

Now the pain
in silent aching separation
— your dignity —

On which gazes
an ageless night's
inscrutable face.

LAMENT FOR THE BELOVED

Was this the only way
you could make
yourself heard,

In so final
a self denial;

All futures gone
in one moment's
furious agony?

* * *

The joys
you left us,

Ours to seek
some meaning in,
the tears hidden
behind the smiles,

The runes
you cast for us
in quiet talking,

And the thoughts
we tinkered with.

* * *

Ideas becoming
the platforms
from which we built
those empires,
now fallen
into ruins.

The losses we bear
and watch
others count.

(For Pamela)

Last night clings
to your room
in quiet disarray;

That outside midday
has scorched
— then sealed —
into the shadows;

Those slow words
you spoke and
their sleepy thoughts
they brought back to us,

In greying dawn's
first light
you then took
to bed with you.

And in scented peach
we watch raw summer
spill over the tidy
spaces you left,

Where underwear
now bursts
from suitcases
across naked carpet ...
at your journey's end.

LEAVING

(For Pamela)

You flung your smile
around our bodies
and over morning's
stinging cold,

And mellowing the air
eye scorching —
between us;

Your sunrise said 'take care,'

And with it you took
the best of spring
in your raised 'pyjama-ed' hand;

Flourishing futures un-revealed
you clasped those joys
not yet fulfilled,

In the last of the night
you waved away,
farewells into morning;

Fell into our one
remaining thought
we left clinging
to cold moist day;

'Don't forget to call.'

'I won't,'
my journey said,
as life moved on
another breath.

LOVE HURTS

you said
and plunged your thoughts
into my soul
— words —
burning to the hilt,
palled over our no-man's-land;
our stale victories hanging
unvanquished in the air.

Now,
we clear the debris
— the casualties —
and the fallen cathedrals
we had built around us,
and sought our refuge in.

And,
collecting the petals
of our broken promises —
                    yet our love ...

we poured honey
into our wounds.

LOVE POEM

We
who consummated
our pagan rites
the night spread out for us,
between linen walls
— ransacked —

Sleep banished
tarnished to tingling tiredness —

And sheets discarded
in passion's nakedness of night,
this we left
stripped bare
        — immodestly —

And this we celebrated
— consecrated love —
we who devoured — ravenously —
each other,

Like the dry season's thirsting
for those its first rains
— and swims —
in huge gulps of lust.

* * *

Now the darkness;
its star peered in,
and in astonishment
blinked on love
consummate.

LOVE IS ...

the rainy days
that remember you,
the way you
caught the sun
and kept it for me,
and let your hair
speak in the long
slow colours of a
summer's evening;

... at a whim
once blonde, now henna
through raven
and into twilight's
darkest most distant
night;

... and your smile
that stayed to
greet the stars and say
'come hither',
ours this moment,
this eternity;

... and how you balanced
all we ever had
on your lips;

... that is love's unspoken word

... ours was the kiss.

MORNING AFTER

Here the ashes lie
amid last evening's conversation,
stale, stubbed out
in the earliest hours.

Now the scent of the spent cigarette.

A sallow light sulks around
into morning's cold corners,
where the table lamps wilt
and amber pales,

Into cool grey, chilly memory.

MUM AND DAD

The door closes — and quietly —
as you walk away,

The whispering in the trees
are the last words you leave;

Now softly in the air
they linger,

As all you said
finds its place — its peace.

NIGHT OUT ON THE TOWN

Glasses chimed the passing hour
toasting conversation
that sought the night's small places
the music left,

Between songs for the heavy hearted.

And slurring over all we spoke
ice chinked — shivered —
into new drinks poured,

Soothing the words
the cigarette smoke kneaded
in spiralling ecstasy ...

These a gaudy night
slipped into her hand,
on a chink of light
and half a song that slipped
through a door, left ajar.

The evening drained
its last applause,
then put out the lights;

Ours was the laughter
the empty streets brandished,
and that led us home
on songs the music
had left us with.

OLD TRACTORS NEVER DIE

The Fordson has furrowed its last,
left lame on a tireless wheel,
and trailing gulls chase after
a younger generation
— eager hands scavenging
what might be saved;

Where the thistle claims
its obscure victory
in this corner the nettle stings,
and the bramble ploughs its way
over the bones of the beast.

To these abandoned years
a harrow adds some
well hidden neglect,
dug into soil,
it is powerless to turn.

Old tractors never die
just — rust to dust — become
part of the fields they ploughed.

OLD WALLS

... that captivate
their many woes
now even time defiles,

Casts anew the figure of a man
flesh and blood cut into morning,
heralds the crossing of the seasons,
as spring invades and rampant sun
purges the last damp dark corners
a winter seeks in its trauma of
retreating cloud.

The wars that wore this place
to crumbling stone
brute elements now torment;

The shrieking rains a winter
scorches to its summers that sear;
and wound this place with its past.

And us ...?
What of we who seek
some order to things
in the flaming Arab consonants
the risen sun picks out;
where once the castellated gate
held the lands
these crumbling stones now crown?

PLATRES

Summer's on the rampage
and raises its earth spirits,
hectic stone shred to scree,
crimps, creeping across
bruised veins of colour;

Deep ochre rustling
into the shadows of trees
gathered around
their fallen needles;

The pines
that scratch their living
from the villages they sweep
to the sides of the road.

* * *

And surefooted scrub
scrambles deftly
over sheer rock
scattering the summer
deep into valleys,
sweet with shade;

Where sparse winter lies
— and where it fell —
the sun now curls
around the corners
of the day.

And the passing hills
climb their dry paths
to where the torrents of winter
are parched to
well worn tracks,

Of that last rain
which fell into
clinging mountain air,
among the voices of the trees,

Now 'sylphing' down
— among muses — spirits —
with what breeze they catch,
the way the roads lead,

These secrets of the summer
through their sleeping trees.

POEM

(For Pamela, with love)

I've heard of that war;

Again I heard of it;
it was in your voice,
your words taking cover
seeking their foxholes
deep in your mind,
at the other end
of the telephone line.

Your feelings tethered
tightly around him,
held as close as love ever can.

And I felt you bleed
into the tension,
as any of the war's wounded;
turning such a young face,
that of a girl
into a woman.

POPPY DAYS

She stood entrenched against the weather
barricaded behind the warm words
carrying her man's war memories
into the sleeting rain;
feeling the weaknesses
in our waterproofs,
coarse November outflanked
the windcheaters us bystanders wore;

We who hunkered down
round the voice of frail memory,
chattering with cold.

Within earshot of the past he talked,
we seized the gaps between the clouds
and the smattering of sun
picking on puddles
glistening — wide eyed — up at
the day which wore its gallantries
pinned to thinning tweed
— blazers 'serge-ing' blue —
breast pockets braided
with regimentals.

She brushed a spot of rain
from his shoulder,
and we paused — as he remembered.

SCRAP YARD

I like the scrap yard's
melancholy lie
of metal all worn and wounded.

There's poetry in this ...
the exhausted.

Labour's dying sigh it shares
with the uncouth grass
all wild like a prophet's beard.

The rust that blemishes the last
colours a limp sun simpers around,
tarnish throttling at the last
moments of some faded livery.

That tired surrender, steel to weed,
and wood to twisted grass,
this dying beast of man's ingenuity,
decaying to dust.

Now the ghost of some deceased
diesel engine splutters in the shadows,
are they the hands that wrought
so many hours of work from this,

Or the wild thorn scraping
along its corroded ribs,
that tells the sneering lie of life?

Here there is some strange dignity
in this most undignified demise.

SEPTEMBER

As the jackdaws
pillage the evening sky
their scrawny caw calls hoarsely
silhouetted against the
dour settling of autumn scores — squalls.

And we settle deeper
huddled towards our mugs
teeming with tea,
as the world unfurls its tragedies in teletext,
over a plate laid waste
with Battenburg.

And somewhere, at the back of our mind,
there's an island
rich with fudge coloured stone
where evening lingers
over a land
of forgotten sleeping gods,

And incense rich
of sweet wine — drips —
and we can taste the past
among the fading shadows,

Where,
not a screech is there
in that clear, clean, air
to stir us.

SOCCER IN THE FOOTHILLS

We climbed the afternoon's narrow ways
settling into soil the muleteer's tracks
trodden by the camel train,
now driven hard into roads;

The gleaming macadam
brings the peaks down
from their lazy cloud
to a car's journey away.

You ahead, leading the way,
and the dust between us;
past rough iron roofs
that nail their mandras into hillsides,

Up to where the promise of rain
weighed heavily on the hills
and the climbing Pefkos—Lefka trees
claw the inclines
looking back down on the game.

The green absorbing the passion,
wives on the perimeter line — cheering —
lime-white lines kicked crooked
by their voices;

Till the hills then thundered
into darkness — into night.

SPRING

... shakes off the soiled silk of winter
and the long drone
of wind around the eaves

— Dies in a splash!

Vivid sunlight recalls
her Sylphs — Nereids —
calls back her sleeping colour,

This morning elemental
from beneath banal grey,
now seeps from waking earth.

And birdsong shrills
high in her still naked trees,
courts the Satyr's dance
that sweeps away the rugged cold
— Euros's harsh work from the East —

Dark those days he left us with
and paths still in the lie
of sweeping drifts of leaves,
that crashing timber
brought to earth
— the trees we knew as boys —

Now gently feels a pulse
hers in a life
that bare earth brings
back from unruly winter,

And all those wounds
that these dark months left
heal across in flowing green.

STAYING UP LATE

We talked till late
while the music cooled
to a tremor
at the back of our thoughts;

And rippled
simmering against
the words we spoke.

Then;

When we had emptied
the night's rich purse
across the dark
waters of time,

You laid out
your dreams for me,
tracing star signs
across the table top.

SUMMERS

We rolled in grass
till we too
smelt of summer.

Long evenings laughing
dripped from our brows
as we ran the length
of the setting sun,

To where evening ached
and cooling stung, chill,
against our exhausted limbs;

And play tired to twilight
then soothed in its soapy water,
rolled nights into
fresh fields of linen;

Folding sleep
over our last words spoken
... into morning.

SUMMER'S MORNING

Morning spreads out its fleece,
purloined gold from the sleeping gods,
a hero's haul, smoothed out;

As now the Olympians' loss
wears the sheer light
of molten summer
— treasure for its seas,

And ruffling at the fringes,
the shoreline paces out
the quiet talk walkers share,

As our past histories
spin out into the deeps;
and lie awake — awash —

Our dreams, fires
flickering in the fleece of gold.

SYRIA

The lands of Arabia
in whispering sands
the Sirocco blows,
across these trodden paths;
theirs the beaten copper — gold —
of silken streets
rich with spice,
where the aroma
of sweet tobacco
stalks the shadows time leaves behind.

Lays these ten thousands of years,
— footprints in the sand —
to climb their hills
towards cloudless summer,
astride the fallen;
castle and crusader's tomb.

Now morning breaks
in a flight of doves
— swiftly — over the hojah's call.

Their caliphs — marauding kings —
theirs the scimitar's flash
and silk woven into time,
dripping the jewels
that legends break like morning
over Arabia's
whispering sands.

THE COFFEE SHOP

The past betrays us;

As octogenarians play out
their patience over green baize,
the cards that hold
in shaking hands,
futures past,
and fortunes won
over harsh words;

That luck then lost
in a change of heart.

As gently curving
the cigarette smoke pales,
unwinding the early morning
towards the ceiling;

Over the talk of the past
and friends long rowed
into halcyon memory,
across the merciless
River Styx.

The past betrays us;

To our greying hair
till we too shall
measure out our memories,
in solitaire;
and patience played out
to the aroma of simmering coffee.

THE RETURN

Between them
no word was spoken;

While jetlag slouched
the tatty corners of the day,
that garrulous greetings
dribbled around,
double crossed — in kisses —

A mother's lipstick
now returning boyhood
bears like a man,

That stubble chinned —
double chinned —
taxi drivers pick up
with the baggage.

No word was spoken — nothing said —

As time caught her
by the hair
flowing — in its stride —
golden folded over
maternal shoulders.

Parental — prenatal — bliss
closed its eyes over
secrets — tears —
the returning child
and woman shared.

The room slept soundly, last night, around us;
sung to sleep by the early hours of the morning,
and we lay in the arms of the music
till the birdsong tapped on our dreams,
squeezed in a Sunday morning,
slipped in between the shutter slats,
to fumble over our rumpled clothes
of love the night before.

They winked back lain among the sleeping
wrapped in that last dance
we took to bed with us;
and lying between our sleeping bodies,
kisses fresh on the brow of dawn,
brought the break of day
beneath our bedroom door.

The words we waged between us
beaten hard as iron — cold;
we battered into ploughshares
and dismembered the walls
a loveless anger had built around us,
our pain hidden within — immured —
and the lips with which
we cursed, we kissed.

The soul streamed
the tears the eye wept,
betrayed by a kiss.

Forgiven.

THUNDER

Spring wept bitterly
in the winter's last
dark angry hour,
the sky's leaden obscenities,
and taken fright shivered
among its paling shadows.

Blossoms in rags lay
dragged around the ankles
of the morning;
and, light fingered,
surrendered to the road's
swirling to the day's drunken rage.

Torn, top to bottom,
the morning crouched low
its terrified stillness nuzzling
the thresholds of our dreams
we pulled high about our heads;
our last tepid embers of sleep.

Bludgeoned and bedevilled
sky cursed its morning,
as we awoke.

VISITING

Threadbare lanes, weaving frayed,
run rings around their villages.

Dust conspires,
catches its passing shower
and congeals, clinging,
to its tyre tracks

— Those passing trophies
it possesses —

And a footprint shows the way
the morning went;

Winter is stale, now — stalled —
the stagnant cold
is grubby around the edges
and longs — longing —
for spring.

This virginal innocence,
a dire earth desires,
craving that lust for the
first flush of blossom blushing.

And stopping mid-thought
catches the dry stone walls
leaning against the tattered breeze
for company ...

These last frayed rags
the winter leaves.

VOICES OF THE PAST

I

Roads uprooted
where weeds stampede
and the sun
thrashes in furious summer
over the agora.

Startled it crumples into history.

A shocked city
falls back on itself
dishevelled in the bewildered
glory of decay.

II

Which we now besiege
— on tip toe —
hacking echoes
out of the silence;
that last word
the harpies snatched
— mid sentence —

Its kiss
and the ageless sigh
that lovers take
their shape around.

As we seek our pasts
lives once lived,
too far away to recall.

We sat and watched
the curious games
autumn likes to play
against the colours
a summer holds sacred, still,

Between the sips of tea
and the pasts we talked away
from the corner of your sorrow.

Late afternoon came
to join us — uninvited —
your words cut across
through the kitchen windows;
half-light wincing into the glare
— frozen in surprise —

The day swung low
and swept down
over our shoulders,
and you turned
the awkward smile
you sheltered your feelings behind,

Bright eyes towards brighter light.

We were drunk,
you and I,
upon the music;

And the dance
led deep into the night's
enchanted places,

Where music quiets
— then hush —
stilled voices become whispers
and words the unspoken touch.

Then dawn comes,
latent upon our last kiss;
and strikes its colours,
Apollo's gold on the brow of the morning;

And the earliest sunlight
sears our bodies
stiff with sleep.

WHERE THE GODS DIED YOUNG

Hot clothes smear
the summit of the day
to lithe limbs panting,
drawing youth
to her girlish figure;

As she picks her way
— tenderly —
over the contours
of the breeze.

To where the gods
died young — here;
met with the
edge of the sword,

And legends now weave
her fair locks, spun
— streaming —

As Apollo from
Hyperborean slumbers,
stirs spring to catch
its breath on a sliver
of his morning.

Then turns
to old age again,
this place;
where the gods
died young — here.

Winter comes in from hiding,
creeping up on autumn's
shrill winds and the rattle
of parched leaves against the dust;

Now, the first rumours
rumble in the foothills
and there's the telltale
whispering in the air;

Of its ill wind that has
September tug at the last
coloured streamers of summer;

As the end of the season
runs for cover and the
thirsting land sighs in prayer,

High on the scent
of damp — drenched — earth,

And we feel the pinch of grey
cloud the sky.

You see,

I am a romantic
and I build my castles
among the stars;

I give them raven floors,
ebony black, to measure
the depth of the night,

And walls of gossamer,
and paper thin dreams,

That in the stillness
brush against the soul's
lonely search for its mate.

* * *

I am a romantic,
you see;

And I wrap the walls
of my world with my dreams.

ZEIMBEKIKO (... and the meaning of flight)

I

The darkness echoed
to the shudder of its stars — shaken —
against our swirling dance;

And cloudless
moonless night
preyed on us — the sleepless,

In our solace of music,
we had unearthed from
the empty air.

II

Where you had taken me,

To that precipice
and looking down
we, upon this night
            — its city.

And you who had taught me
the meaning of flight.

in its eleven easy steps ...

III

'The sky knows its music,'
you said;
'and you have heard its song.'

And there you left me
— with just your smile —
to navigate the night,

till dawn.